MAKING THE LOVE
YOU WANT

MAKING THE LOVE YOU WANT

MIKE JOHNSON

MIKE JOHNSON

Making the Love You Want

Copyright © 2020 Mike Johnson
First edition
Softcover ISBN 978-1-7354001-0-5
Hardcover ISBN 978-1-7354001-1-2

BOOK DESIGN Laura Wrubleski
EDITOR Lori Bamber
PUBLISHING SUPPORT TSPA The Self Publishing Agency Inc.

*Kourtnei, I sometimes wonder what truly lies behind a
smile. Is there sadness and pain? Or pure joy?*

I dedicate my book to you.

*This book is my contribution to the fight against a
growing pandemic of mental illness.*

See you in heaven.

Readers, I truly hope you enjoy the journey we're about to embark on! I wanted every detail of this book to align with the principles of self-love, including its design.

The interior theme and feel are inspired by the Japanese aesthetic, *wabi-sabi*. "Wabi" is said to be defined as an "understated elegance" with a focus on minimalism; "sabi" translates to something like, "taking pleasure in the imperfect."

I believe we humans must learn to love ourselves fully, including every perceived imperfection, and to hold true to that love. Like the ballerina tattoo I have on my forearm, *wabi-sabi* illustrates the astonishing beauty in balance.

Be good to you, and thrive.

CONTENTS

INTRODUCTION

I distinctly remember reaching the point in my life where choosing to love myself was no longer optional.

At first, it was just about having the confidence to claim my place in the world. Eventually, it became a gateway to freedom. It was the key to unlocking the chains my world had placed on my heart, mind and soul.

My sister and I were raised by my mother and grandmother, and as a child, I remember desperately wanting to be a masculine man who could protect our household.

Things weren't always easy. There were difficult moments and faith-defining times, but my mother always did the best she could with what she had. During those trying times, I learned the value and benefit of perspective, positivity and gratitude.

It broke my heart to see the pain in her eyes when she wasn't able to provide the quality of life that she wanted for us. Somehow, even at a very young age, I was aware of our circumstances, and I didn't want my mom to stress over things that weren't in her control. My younger sister, Amber, and I had our fair share of nights on which a 99-cent frozen pizza split between the two of us was dinner, but we knew Mom was doing her best. My mother was and is a shining star of resiliency, determination and persistence, going to great lengths to provide for two kids on her own while miraculously managing to attend college at the same time.

I knew that, like her, I wanted to be the kind of person who lifted other people up. But I battled with my insecurities. They stood in the way of being the man I wanted to be. The man I am.

When I was five, we lived in Germany, and my babysitter sexually assaulted me[1]. My memories of fighting her off me and exploding out the front door to get away are still vivid.

Afterward, I wondered about my sexuality and masculinity. For years I questioned myself: "Why would I fight her off if I'm attracted to women?"

It was emotionally and mentally catastrophic to me. I never told my mom or anyone else what happened. For some reason, I felt that a more masculine man would have handled the situation differently, no matter how young. Although I knew that what happened to me should never happen to any child, I couldn't help but think something was wrong with me.

It was hard work to love myself through these and other insecurities. But as time passed, I grew stronger, with more

---

1 According to the most credible statistics available, somewhere between 30 and 50 percent of girls and 10 to 20 percent of boys are sexually abused by adulthood. If you look around a crowded room, you'll likely be stunned by the number of people you know who have probably experienced that particular complex trauma. Add race-related trauma and trauma related to other forms of violence and it becomes clear that the vast majority of us have brains that are wired for survival rather than thriving. Fortunately, there is an antidote: self-love.

awareness of who I was. Things changed for me. Loving myself saved me.

Self-love was once a catchphrase that fell easily from my lips, but it came to mean the stronghold required for survival.

Before I made self-love my touchstone, devoting endless amounts of energy to others' expectations exhausted me. I became a stranger within my own body. Frozen on the inside, I was dead to the world around me. Yet I showcased a big smile that spoke to the emotions of others.

A friend, raised by a family he hadn't been born into, once told me about his struggle coming to self-love.

He said, "All that I knew was given to me. But all that was given to me was never theirs to give." He felt like an outsider among those he had known almost his entire life because *there was a part of him that was undiscovered*. It was a part of him that he longed to know, a part of himself he felt he needed to explore to truly understand who he was. He felt as if he couldn't love himself without it.

When I finally learned to love myself and committed to choosing my values and desires over those of others, I started to feel like I was able to breathe for the first time. Saying yes to my heart gave me a new outlook on life.

Finally I could breathe life, and life breathed its abundance of grace back into me.

It's my belief that changing your perspective on life is essential to happiness. After all, when people decide to love themselves, their goal is happiness by whatever means they define it. Happiness requires that we develop a positive outlook.

To do so, we must have a clear vision of our world. Gaining access to that vision begins with being honest with ourselves about ourselves. We must demonstrate absolute candor about who we are, including the things we like and dislike about ourselves. More importantly, we must reflect on the things we fear and the qualities and experiences we are ashamed of. These are the aspects of the self that restrict us and prevent us from taking the chances that could shift the momentum of our lives. Our fears and the experiences we are ashamed of hold us back; they are the roots of our stagnation and lack of movement.

We must grow into the courageous acts that generate positive change, something that can only happen if we love ourselves.

It's true that these challenges are rarely, if ever, easily overcome. Our emotional and psychological wounds never heal quickly. Self-shaming can be like lesions that tear open each time we reach for new opportunities.

Reaching our potential takes faith.
Building the life and love we want takes faith.
To have that faith in ourselves, we must love ourselves.

Self-love isn't something anyone else can give you. But when you've discovered the path, you'll find you want to share it with others. That's what happened to me. And that's the purpose of this book.

PART ONE

Discovering Self-Love

I

THE DEFINITION
OF SELF-LOVE

"It was a house without any mirrors, just a reflection of my soul. I wanted to call this place, forever, my home."

B eing free is more than being released from life's external shackles.

Written history shows us that people have been oppressed by the boundaries of others' thinking since the beginning of language, perhaps long before.

Once we have shaken off the shackles the world places upon us, we must shake off the ones we've internalized, the human desire to please anyone other than ourselves.

That doesn't mean we must be selfish. In fact, we can only reach our true potential to contribute to our world when we access our completely unique brilliance. This is only possible with the freedom that self-love ignites.

In college, I read that self-love begins when we observe our own actions and words with compassion. Those words from the Merriam-Webster Dictionary have always stuck with me for some reason. Maybe it's the part about being aware and conscious of ourselves, the decisions we make and things we do. Self-reflection is necessary so that we can get to know and understand ourselves.

Somewhere along the way, the vast majority of us contract a form of Stockholm syndrome, developing a need for acceptance from those who judge us by their standards. Our need to be wanted and accepted by others became greater than our need to be respected and aligned with our own values.

When we look to others to tell us who we are and how we should act, life can go very wrong. We can fall into abusive relationships. Children become enslaved by the unfulfilled expectations of their guardians. Violence plagues economically poor communities worldwide.

There is simply nothing more toxic and dysfunctional than the need to please someone who does not respect, value and love you.

Sadly, so much of our suffering is self-inflicted, the result of feeling the need to fill a void with experiences that stain our hearts. When we make decisions without considering what's best for us, we experience feelings of regret, resentment and even shame.

I know that story well.

The truth is I don't really remember much about my life before the age of 15. My family believes that something traumatic happened and I just blocked it out. They're not wrong.

As I mentioned in the introduction, I was sexually assaulted at age five by a babysitter. I wasn't physically harmed; she took her clothes off while we were playing hide-and-seek and grabbed me, then chased me as I ran. I got away. But the emotional effects were devastating, and a displaced sense of shame stayed with me into adulthood. Trauma research shows that this is a common effect of childhood sexual abuse—because children see the world around them as undivided from themselves, they internalize shame that belongs to others. They grow up feeling that there is something terribly wrong with them, no matter what else they do. The shame, trust issues and damage to our ability to create healthy boundaries can last a lifetime.

As is the case for so many of us—wherever we come from—family violence was also part of my story. I remember my mom falling hard after being pushed by her then-husband and being so angry at myself because I was too small to defend her. My mom's only sister was murdered, and while I was too young to remember it happening, her loss scarred our family forever.

My father wasn't someone I saw often. (My parents never married.) I do remember going to visit my dad once during the summer. He asked me if I knew who he was, and when I said yes, he told me to say it—he wanted me to call him Dad.

I couldn't. Even today, I don't call my father "Dad" when we're together. On Father's Day, I send him a card. I put "To Dad" on it and I say, "Love Mike." He's been a really good father under the circumstances. I love him and we have a great relationship. But for the longest time I held a grudge against him because he wasn't always there. That's not all his fault, of course, but it's one of the reasons I want to be married for life to the woman I have children with.

In sixth grade, we moved from Irving, Texas, to Grand Prairie, Texas, and that's where all but a few of my earliest memories begin. As the new kid, I was teased for being light-skinned and skinny. I wasn't good at jokes or comebacks. I remember getting down on my knees, praying to God to be dark-skinned, to be the color of Wesley Snipes. Where I come from, if you're light-skinned you're considered a bitch. Frail. So I was bullied. It all played into my shame, and my feeling that I just wasn't man enough.

My mom's family lives in Dallas. Once, when I was eight or nine, she dropped me off to get a haircut. When she returned to get me, I was disgusted by the way the men there looked at her, as if she was a piece of meat and they were lions that hadn't eaten for a long time. I felt an uncontrollable, compelling urge to protect her.

My mom tells me that, as a young child, I was often sick and in the hospital a lot. She tells the story of being beside my hospital bed, with my grandmother, when I started talking in my sleep to her sister who had been murdered. I said, "Aunt Tina, I can't go to Heaven with you. I want to stay here and protect Mom, Amber and Grandma." Years later, I still get chills thinking about that—it's always been in me, that desire to be my best so I can be of service to the people I love.

It took me a while to find that man.

Teenagers test the values they are taught, and I was no different. My first job was at McDonald's and I walked two miles there and two miles home. I got a second job as well, just trying to make more money. At McDonald's, I was an extremely fast cashier, good with numbers, and so they put me on the back window. Thousands of people came by the back window and, if they ordered two things off the dollar menu, it cost $2.17 with tax. They'd give me $3; I knew automatically that their change was 83 cents but instead I'd give them 53 cents and drop 30 cents in my pocket. I told myself it was a smart way to boost my minimum wage.

I even started to think about selling weed. But the day I made the decision to go ahead, the sniffing dogs came to my school. I realized I was more terrified of getting caught and breaking my mom's heart than I was of not having enough cash.

I started to gain confidence when I was playing football in my senior year of high school. I was backup; one day during practice, the starter told the coach he wasn't going to run a play because he wasn't going to get the ball. The coach told me to run the play instead and that just that switched something in me so hard. I got pissed off. I was working my butt off, too, trying to get better, and I said, "If I go in for this play, you better throw me the ball." They threw me the ball and I caught it.

That event changed my compass. Tension had built up in me for so many years and I was just finally fed up. I was fed up with not being confident. I was fed up with being overlooked. I realized that I had to know my own worth and step into that worth.

Then they put me in a game—and I couldn't catch for nothing. I dropped the ball and my confidence shattered. I looked into the stands and saw one of the cheerleaders, Laura

Roberts, a friend. I remember the disappointed expression on her face to this day.

Self-love is a winding up-and-down journey, one that each one of us must travel on our own.

After football season, it was time to start preparing for colleges and I asked my mom if she would write my application letters and essays. She looked at me like I was crazy.

I said, "Mom, all the other kids have their parents write their letters and essays!"

She said, "Mike, now you got to be yourself."

Peoples' infidelity to the truth is often accompanied by their love affair with lies. The more comfortable a person becomes with their lies, the more likely they are to accept them. In the end, the impact of no longer recognizing the truth is worse than any displeasure you might endure because of telling the truth.

A friend of mine once told me about a dream he had in which he met himself for the first time.

"There was a room that looked completely foreign to me but also felt familiar. My mind ran through my memories, but I could not figure it out. It bothered me. I opened the door and walked around; I realized there was not one mirror in the entire house.

"I thought, how could anyone live without ever seeing

themselves?" he said.

Listening to him, I thought about how I'd wondered the same thing. How can we live without seeing ourselves clearly?

My friend went on to tell me that the house he dreamed about had a different way of helping people see themselves. Each room held a memory of something good, something longed for and attained. A moment in life when the Earth stood still for him and he fell in love with that precise moment. Whenever it was, wherever it was, if he was there, in that moment, he was good.

As he talked, I realized that this is the way I think about self-love.

You have to be willing to tell yourself the truth in order to love yourself. You have to be willing to live your truth.

When I was a teenager, I knew I sometimes let my mom down. It was when I was older, more mature, that I realized I was letting myself down too. Being able to accept that truth allowed me to think about who I want to be in the world and to work hard every day to be that person.

Self-love is looking at yourself with compassion. But it is also being honest with yourself and applying discipline, honesty and your own values to everything you do.

There are moments when I think I've just about got self-love right, and then this thing called life happens. I find myself once again picking up the pieces.

I don't think loving yourself is something you ever perfect, but it's important that you remain in constant pursuit. It is the key to everything else you want to achieve, believe me, whether it is being happy, being a leader in your community, making money, finding the love of your life or being a good parent.

When you can't figure out how to love yourself or you lose sight of how to do so, life is a constant struggle. You can be swallowed up by everything or anyone.

Another friend of mine put this way: "I was an empty bucket, always looking to others to fill me up. When they said good things about me, I felt great. When they talked trash, I felt worthless. Now my bucket is full—what other people say and do is like rain on the ocean if I'm right with myself."

We all lose our way sometimes on stormy nights and wash up on the foreign shores of others' expectations. Some people get so lost that they never see another sunrise.

It doesn't have to be like that. Self-love is your own North Star. Your longings are whispers from your heart; pleasing you is the gateway to your happiness.

I've lost count of how many times I have asked, "How do I love myself?"

Some people would say self-love is happiness, contentment, acceptance and honesty. The renowned American author, professor, feminist and social activist bell hooks writes, "We would all love better if we used it as a verb."

Real love is not a feeling but a foundation for action. When we love someone else, their happiness is as important to us as our own. When we love ourselves, we love the person we are today, and we love our future self; we are willing to do whatever is necessary to take care of the person we are building with our current actions.

We all have our own definition of what self-love means, depending on who we want to be, what we need and what we want out of life. I have found peace in my own translation. After all, we can only see with the eyes we were given.

Loving yourself is what you make it. It's completely up to you how you choose to demonstrate that love. No one has the right or authority to suggest otherwise. But whatever you see inside yourself, whatever you call love, however you define it, it must be rooted in honesty.

Self-love rooted in honesty will grow into confidence, the kind that doesn't have to look around for validation. We were all created equal and worthy, and each of us offers something entirely unique to this world. When you know who you are, and you love that person fully, you are truly present to the people around you. You're not unconsciously asking, "Who do you think I am? How do you feel about me?" You become the kind of person who brings calm, wisdom and love wherever you go.

Our colorful blue planet is populated by infinite possibilities because each of us has the potential to be a divine blessing if we choose to.

But our focus must be in the right direction.

I encourage you not to look out into the world, but rather within.

Take a beat. Get quiet. Look into your soul, your you-ness. Focus on the changes you can create. Love yourself so deeply that you come to understand that the world needs you at least as much as you need the world.

So many people wonder how to begin, but it's simple. Don't look at what the world can offer you, but at what you can offer the world. Be so in touch with your inner self that you can feel it creating positive change in the world. When you tap into your fundamental nature and keep that channel open, the restraints of the world cannot hold you back.

Your Action Item

When I was a kid, my elders would say to me, "You can lead a horse to the water, but you cannot make it drink." Right?

I can tell you what I needed to do to love myself, but it's not my place to tell you how to love you. As kindred spirits in hope, we must define ourselves by our own measures.

I can guarantee you that if you choose to start loving yourself, you will harvest fruitful blessings.

You know that feeling when you wake up and feel so great that you realize feeling "normal" is incredibly wonderful? Sometimes it happens after you've been sick, or a few months after a bad breakup. It's like you can see for the first time. Everything looks so new, vibrant and full of life. So beautiful.

Now imagine you're in this state right now.

You walk past a mirror and catch a glimpse of a you that you don't quite recognize, a you who is lit up brightly from within.

If you're like most of us, you usually walk quickly past mirrors. It's like we're children creeping past our parents' bedroom door after doing something bad, hoping that if we don't look in, they won't see us either.

In the same way, we think that if we don't look at the mirror for long, we won't have to see the bits of ourselves we don't like.

Today, though, dare to boldly confront your insecurities. Investigate.

You'll notice that you are surprisingly beautiful. You are perfect just the way you are.

You don't need to change a thing.

Can't see it? Look longer.

Imagine you've learned to see yourself for who you are, and to love what you see.

Maybe you never knew how much you liked the lines in your smile, the melody of your voice and the comfort of your own company.

"Where have you been? Why didn't I notice you before?" you ask, with your warmest smile on your face.

"Where have you been? I needed you!"

Just like that, we stumble upon a golden truth: the person we need most is ourselves.

All we ever needed was waiting inside of us this entire time, waiting for us to be brave enough to look with the eyes of love.

Sometimes loving yourself is realizing that you need yourself and no one else.

Don't get me wrong. The stronger your relationships with your family and community, the more you'll be able to accomplish. But none of that matters until you are there for yourself first of all.

I am so fortunate to be surrounded by a loving circle of strong people. They continuously provide me with the support I need to move forward in my life.

Still, I make room for solitude, and these moments are an extremely important part of my growth. Not taking the time to reflect on our thoughts and emotions and to organize them into a framework for our lives can have dire consequences.

Now's the time to decide: will you make time for the most important person in your life? (Yes, that's you.) Even if it is just a 10-minute check-in with your morning coffee, or before you shut off the light at night, you'll soon find it to be the most productive time of your day in terms of creating real change.

Schedule it now. Pull out your phone or wherever you manage your calendar and mark it in.

There. You're on your way.

Your Life, Starring the One and Only You

We cannot be what someone else wants us to be even if we try. At some point, who we are, even from a genetic point of view, will undeniably overcome who we try to be. Trying to be someone else takes so much effort and energy that largely goes to waste.

Being you? Well, it feels so damn good, so liberating. And the energy you put into loving you? It's a high-return investment on your future self, your future life.

There are moments when the only voice we need to listen to is our own. It's important to recognize these times because, ultimately, we are the ones who must live with the consequences of our decisions.

Sure, our actions do impact those around us, some more than others. The impact could very well be devastating, depending on the relationship.

Nevertheless, I think my mother summed it up best.

"Mike, you make your bed, now you have to lay in it, son!"

When we are entrenched in satisfying other people, even when we finally experience the spiritual release of being ourselves, it's not always easy to decide which is more important.

For some, it's our hearts' desires. For others, it's the expectations of people they are emotionally invested in. But when you truly understand what it means to love yourself, you also understand what it means to trust yourself. As self-love becomes the lens through which you see yourself and your life, you develop the gift of discernment—sound judgment and clarity. You gain access to a new mindset. You understand that all you can do in this world is be yourself. As the wise ones say on Instagram, everyone else is already spoken for.

Loving yourself is part of our journey in this world. It's part of the puzzle of you, of creating the best version of yourself.

First, we have to define self-love for ourselves.

How do we want other people to treat us? Is that what we are teaching them through the way we treat ourselves?

Your Action Item

You know, what I like about mirrors the most is not that I can see how I look. I know what I look like. But there are other things our reflection can offer us.

Clarity.

Truth.

Let us do something together to seek the truth buried within us. Find a mirror in your home. It doesn't matter if it's small or large.

In the mirror, look deeply into your eyes. Keep looking until you find something inside of you that is beautiful.

Now, find some paper and write down what you believe self-love is. Write a short description of what it means to you. Ignore what other people may have said and even what you've read in this book.

This is about your experiences, your thought processes and your growth.

Close your eyes. Take a deep breath and release. Let your emotions and thoughts flow freely through the pen onto the paper. I encourage you not to hold back. Write what you feel.

Set yourself free.

Once you finish, do not change anything or question yourself.

Next, I want you to take the paper and read what you've written out loud to yourself three times. Each time, speak louder and more boldly. Speak with confidence. Let the words flow through you and roll off your tongue.

Listen to your heart and allow yourself to believe what it tells you about yourself.

Now take a moment. Meditate on your own words and give yourself permission to accept your truth about self-love.

Finally, take the paper and place it on the back of the mirror. Leave it there for when you need it to remind yourself of who you are and what you believe about yourself.

I want you to remember these words, your words. Whenever you look in the mirror, whether it is a quick glance or another deep conversation with yourself, I encourage you to do so with this new outlook.

The image in the mirror should now serve as a reminder: You are so much more than the dimples in your smile or the color of your eyes. The physical gifts from God that we all possess do not define us.

From now on, when you pass the mirror, look first for your light. It's there—the only one like it in the universe. Self-love is the way you keep it burning bright.

Self-Love Mantra

Self-love is about me.

It's not about them.

This time I choose.

And I choose me.

Today, I choose what I desire and what I need.

I let go of other's expectations.

No longer will I live in the shadows of recommendations.

I will listen to my heart.

I choose to define my own happiness.

I am enough.

I love my body.

I love my mind.

I love my soul.

I love all of me.

(*Say your name*), I love you

Self-love, power and growth arise from the ashes of continuous pursuit and hardships.

Love yourself!

It doesn't matter if you feel like no one else does, **you love you and that's enough.**

II

SELF-REFLECTION

As soon as you wake up, stumble into the bathroom. Look into the mirror before you open your eyes to the wider world.

You are the first thing you see, a field of consciousness that exists before thoughts enter your mind.

That's you. Right there.

Look!

After high school, I started community college, paying for it out of the money I'd made working. It was all we could afford, and after a while, when the money ran out, I dropped out because I didn't want to go into debt.

I had a conversation with my uncle about my options. He asked, "Mike, what's going to make you a man the fastest?"

It seemed clear that the answer to my uncle's question was joining the airforce full time. But I wouldn't end up doing that until I was almost 22.

Instead I got an apartment with a friend; my mom didn't speak to me for three months because I'd moved out.

In many ways it was a nightmare, but it was during those next three years that I really started learning about who I am and what I need to do to be a great man.

Near the end of that period, I sank into an extreme depression. I left my apartment, went to my mom's house and went to bed. I was working at Walmart and I stopped going in. I didn't even call in sick. I had a girlfriend, but I stopped calling her.

My mom would come home after work and ask if I was okay, but I didn't want to talk at all. The TV would be on, but I was never watching TV.

I kept saying my date of birth and my social security number to myself, over and over again. I feel like the reason was that I didn't want to lose my identity and felt that I was. Day after day, I laid in bed, seldom eating. Finally my mom was so scared that she took me to the hospital—the psychiatric ward. They connected wires to my head to try to figure out what was wrong with me.

Eventually we were told that I had a dissociative disorder, a condition that is common among survivors of complex trauma. The doctors weren't sure what to do.

I went home. I didn't want to take medicine.

I've never been one to be disrespectful to my mom. Yet one time during this period, when she asked me how I got into this state, I looked at her coldly and said, "What, the state of Texas? I don't know. You brought me here."

It was so rude of me. I knew what she meant, and I didn't know how to answer her question. My personality had shifted, and I didn't know why.

I do remember the moment I snapped out of it. I was at my dad's house and there was a music video on. I don't remember what was playing, but it was almost as if there was a click and I figured out in that moment who Mike Johnson is.

I realized that I tend to become extremely depressed if I am not progressing in life; I forget who I am as a person.

I suddenly understood that I have to keep striving in order to take care of myself, to love myself.

Friends who know me well say that I will get whatever I strive for. I believe that's because I've figured out who I am. I figured out who I am by hitting rock bottom, and the man I am is also the reason I hit rock bottom.

Don't get me wrong. You do not have to hit bottom to get to know and love yourself, to be true to the person you are. But many of us have been there. Shame about those experiences can keep us down, or we can use our bottom as a springboard.

I'm here to tell you there is a way back. Let me tell you about the reasons that got me there.

I was working at Walmart, and I had a second job at a gas station. Before that, I'd been, as we called it, hitting licks: robbing homes and passing electronics off to friends so they could pawn them. I was 6'4", 165 pounds, and getting into fights left and right. I would go to a fast-food restaurant and throw a package of ketchup at the cashier, taunting him to fight me. I had an attitude problem, a wild rock star crazy streak. I was having sex as if women were becoming extinct.

From 18 to 21, I was not the man my mother raised me to be. I was not the man I wanted to be. I was not the man *I am*.

Finally, the man I am snapped, and I fell into depression and dissociative disorder.

I had been living for others, fitting in, surviving. I didn't know who I was becoming, and I knew if I stayed on that road, nothing good would happen.

On the Tuesday before I left for military training, my friends and I came out of a nightclub and someone started shooting at us. No one was hit, miraculously, and to this day I don't know who was shooting at us or why.

What changed my life at that time was a line in a song by a rapper named Plies. "Is two years of balling worth going 10 years a fed for?" (Meaning federal penitentiary.)

I could see that future ahead of me.

A decade has passed now. I'm sharing this with you honestly because it is that period of my life that makes it possible for me to empathize with those who are on the wrong path today.

I could easily be labeled a felon right now, easily. And in America, when you're a felon, it's almost impossible to come back from. I have lots of friends who are in that position.

I let myself down, and I let my family down. But in the end, I got lucky. I understand now that my behaviors during that time were consistent with what psychologists understand about the effects of trauma. If I'd known, or my friends and family had known, it's possible I could have turned things around earlier.

Don't get me wrong: I don't mean I robbed homes because my babysitter abused me, or my mom's husband shoved her around, or my aunt was murdered.

I'm saying what scientists have proven, that trauma changes the brain. The survival system dial gets turned up to 10 and the cerebral cortex, the center of our higher thought and self-control, goes offline.

When this happens, bad decisions invariably get made.

"Make good choices?" When the brain is in survival mode, there are no good choices—there is only fight, flight or freeze.

These experiences taught me to never judge someone by their labels or their circumstances.

I have since learned the value of effective self-reflection, the way we get to know ourselves intimately. It's an essential element in the process of building the life we want. It isn't easy, but the effort should never be abandoned.

Self-love is impossible to attain if we don't look inward. We can't gain access to our inner selves without our own involvement. Each day I dig deeper, unveiling another part of my self. Truthfully, I don't always like what I see. But it's a requirement for healing and moving past things in my life that have been holding me back.

What I find astonishing is that, more than 10 years into this process, I am still learning things about myself that I had forgotten or didn't know in the first place.

It's All Food for Growth

Self-reflection is a method used by accomplished people from all walks of life.

If you look at athletes, for example, they regularly reflect on their previous efforts. They look to identify things that they did right and wrong, finding important lessons in both. Self-reflection is not about whether something is good or bad. It's about improvement, nothing more than that.

You can be sure that elite fighters like Claressa Shields don't skip past the parts of tournament videos in which they do something well. At the same time, they don't become obsessed with the parts where they make mistakes. I'm sure they carefully examine the things they did well so they can execute even more meticulously the next time. They reflect on the mistakes they made to prevent them from happening again, or to at least improve their chances of not repeating them. Either way, they can't improve something that they are not aware of. They learn about their habits; they learn more about themselves each time they use self-reflection. They become more adept at executing on their goals.

This applies to us all, even if we are not elite athletes or star performers.

We are human beings first, each of us searching for happiness by improving our lives and ourselves. Examining your own life and analyzing the things you do and say are necessary components of self-reflection. It's not about what you do for a living, but who you want to be while you are living. Self-reflection helps make you a better friend, parent, partner or colleague.

Look inside of yourself and accept what you see. Then take steps to brighten that image by polishing away the parts that are not you. This process will enhance your ability to love yourself more intimately.

Finding Your Why

While I was in college, our teachers would routinely have us perform reflection activities after completing a project. For the longest time, I thought this was completely useless. Like most people, I focused solely on results. At times, when my knowledge in a subject did not improve, I became frustrated and upset. Why was I not improving the way I thought I should? In my eyes, I was putting in the work, studying hard, and completing my assignments to the best of my ability. For the life of me, I could not understand what was happening.

One day my teacher asked me why I never participated in the reflection activities.

My answer was simple. "It isn't part of my grade."

It couldn't change what I'd already done, I said. I was honest with her. "In my opinion, it is a waste of time."

"Are you telling me that if something doesn't change what you have already done, it's not part of the process of improvement?" she asked.

Sadly, I was too young and inexperienced to understand her then. But I understand her now.

What I failed to realize back then was that, in reflection, I discover new truths.

Finally, frustrated, I decided to try reflection after one of my projects.

"Let's just try it out and see what happens," I thought. "It can't do any more damage than what was already done, right?"

The content of the reflection exercise took me by surprise. It didn't focus on things like, "Did you study?" or "How long did you study for?" Instead, it asked questions such as:

+ "Do you enjoy this class?"

+ "Why did you choose to take this class?"

+ "What do you expect to gain from taking this class?"

+ "Are you confident in your ability to reach your desired outcomes in this class?"

+ "Is your work ethic and commitment reflected in your preparation each day for this class?"

I was in awe! When I talked to the teacher about it, she said that I obviously knew how to study because I made it into college. I would not be there if I didn't demonstrate in high school that I had earned that right and could perform on a higher academic level.

Reflecting in this way is not about measuring ourselves against external standards, but about fueling our sense of purpose.

If we don't know *why* we are doing what we are doing, we have a problem. We can easily lose focus and ourselves in the process. We can put ourselves in a position that is extremely complicated to escape. How many of us have said something like, "We met, we started talking. Before I knew it, we were together."

We look for a temporary way to support our family and then keep showing up to work at a job we hate, year after year, until it becomes an unshakeable routine.

"I am just used to it," or "This is how it is," we say.

If you find yourself in this situation, remember: Your purpose creates your ambitions; your ambition inspires your aspirations.

Our aspirations are the emotional language of our desires for our lives. Responding to our aspirations is the essence of what makes us happy and completes us as human beings.

Over 3,000 years ago, the Delphic oracle Pythia is said to have spoken to the Greek God Apollo about "knowing thyself."

Humans have always sought to understand ourselves and exceed our limitations. Whether we call it introspection or self-reflection, it is the examination and analysis of our thoughts and consciousness. It is examining the desires we see at our core and identifying the barriers that keep us from acting on them.

In other words, it isn't enough to just look inside ourselves. We have to be honest, to investigate ourselves thoroughly. Take the time to really consider who you are and what makes you, you. Asking the hard questions forces you to confront anything that you have not moved past, anything that is holding you back.

Do you love yourself enough to cross-examine yourself?

Please don't confuse this process with judging yourself. The world has done that enough. The aim is for you to question your own motivations and actions, then give yourself feedback on how you feel about your decision-making in life thus far.

Your Action Item

I want you to take a moment now.

Pause.

Just breathe. Count backwards from 10 to one, then exhale.

Begin.

Repeat, and as you exhale, think about what you wanted to accomplish during the past week. We are not going to go too far back in time just yet. Let's take a small step and think about this past week alone.

Find a piece of paper. I want you to write down 10 things that you wanted to accomplish this past week. If you don't have 10 things, write down whatever you can. Even if it's just one thing, please, write it down.

Next to each line, put a check mark if you have achieved this goal.

Now, turn over the paper and write a short reflection about each item.

- Why did you want to do it in the first place?
- If you did it, what motivated you?
- Has doing it made you a better person or made your life better?

Next, reflect on any challenges you may have encountered this week. How did those experiences impact you as you pursued your goals?

For each thing you accomplished, think about why you didn't quit. For each thing you didn't, think about what stopped you.

When you finish, place the piece of paper in a drawer. Take another and write down 10 things you want to accomplish in the coming week.

At the end of each week, go through this process again, from beginning to end.

When a month has passed, go back and reflect on your goals for that period. Look at how much you have grown. Imagine what you can accomplish in six months or a year with commitment and dedication to yourself.

I can promise you that you will be amazed at how fulfilling life is when it's built upon loving yourself.

Self-Reflection Mantra

The mirror is empty.

But the image is clear.

I see myself, for myself.

My happiness is here.

I look within.

Not out of.

I look within.

To see the reflection of my self-love;

To see what self-love really is.

———————

You will eventually
understand that **all you
can do in this world is
be yourself.**

III

AWARENESS

To say you know me completely is like buying a painting that the artist has not yet finished. All you can say is that you are aware of some parts of me that have experienced life up until now. As for who I will be tomorrow? I cannot even begin to be known until the day ends.

S elf-reflection is vital. Yet it is only part of the model that enables us to truly love ourselves.

Going a step deeper, we begin to recognize the importance of being aware of what motivates our actions. Awareness stimulates a heightened experience of discovery.

Once we have become aware of what emotions and thoughts lie beneath our actions, once we understand who we are, progressive change is inevitable. Being aware triggers the thinking that drives physical change through redirection and action.

We then live in a state of awareness, an essential condition of true success.

A good friend of mine says that, if we have awareness, we should educate others on it, but if we don't possess it, we should seek it. In her process of self-reflection, she says, she is able to experience her past in her present, while envisioning her future at the same time. Awareness is 360-degree insight into who we are and the life we want.

Once you understand your thinking and are aware of the impact it has had on you throughout life's stages, you can act with freedom and power. You can apply your intelligence and act on your desires to create change.

Ascending to a higher degree of awareness, you begin to re-experience and *understand* your acts of love, hate, jealousy, lack of confidence and any other emotions that have surfaced through your actions. You will understand why you have done the things you have.

Once you understand your past actions, you can forgive yourself. You can forgive others, understanding that they too have made mistakes out of fear and confusion. You can stop trying to educate others who choose not to grow. You can accept where you are in life and develop a strategic thinking process that will improve your position.

Conversely, if you are not aware of the influences that drive you, you are likely to repeat destructive actions in the near or distant future. You can't simply just say you want to do better and think that history won't repeat itself.

Organizing new direction is the practice of using awareness to manage the emotions and habits behind previous mishaps and successes.

When the Light Comes On

When reflecting, you may notice some trends.

You may tend to fall into similar situations.

Have you ever asked yourself, "What the hell was I thinking?" Almost all of us have. But not everyone takes the time to actually answer their own question.

Coming into awareness is like a light bulb coming on in your mind, illuminating the darkness. Suddenly you can see clearly.

It may feel like you have been in the dark forever, repeatedly being hurt, with no chance of relieving the pain. Once the light is turned on, you learn that you've been hurting yourself because so many things were not what or where you thought they were. There is no monster under the bed.

You realize that no one has been stopping you from being you and fulfilling your dreams. No one has the power to stop you.

It's all clear when the light comes on.

Don't get me wrong: there are lots of systems in place designed to keep us small, to keep us afraid. Oppression is real, and its effects are devastating. But whatever happens outside of us, when the light comes on inside, we can be ourselves. We can keep striving toward our dreams. We can decide how to respond to those systems, and we can love ourselves despite them.

That light, awareness, is an experience of revelation.

At some point, you'll even find yourself being able to see through other peoples' poker faces and the smoke and mirrors of deception.

I know you may be thinking the same thing I did at first: "Why?"

Well, when you reach a state of awareness through self-reflection, your brain operates differently than when you made the decisions you're now looking back on. You may have been in the darkness all this time, but you had a switch in your mind ready to turn on the light.

If you are not in a state of awareness, it is very difficult to recognize the truth. Few people do.

What is the truth?

The truth is that *you* are the savior that you have been waiting for.

Awareness brings a conscious awakening that infuses clarity into your thinking. Your limited sight becomes clear vision.

Your inability to be loved in the way you want was a problem you had the answer to all along. With awareness, you realize you have the ability to make the love you want.

Our awareness becomes our reality. It can create or remove boundaries in our minds and physical lives.

The World You Make

Just before the period known as the Age of Enlightenment, a time when thinkers were fixated on philosophy and intellect, there was a remarkable philosopher named Rene Descartes. Born in the late 1500s, a mathematician and scientist, he was credited with making the connection between algebra and geometry. However, his widest fame came from an investigation he conducted when philosophers believed no one could be certain that what they knew was real. Reflecting on himself and his experiences, doubting it was possible to prove that anything at all existed, even himself, he had an epiphany.

"I think, therefore I am."

In other words, I know I exist because someone or something must be doing the thinking.

This spark of awareness was the dawn of a new era. If I doubt myself, then the doubt is real, because I am the one doubting.

With our thoughts, we create our world.

As the old saying goes, people who say they can and people who say they can't are both correct.

You can and will do whatever you set your mind to. You won't rise to the occasion and demonstrate your greatness if you believe that you will fail.

It doesn't matter who else believes in you if you don't believe in yourself.

This is the power of awareness. The human mind is such a miraculous phenomenon. When we focus on how we can love ourselves better, one day at a time, the rewards are truly infinite.

Your Action Item

Tomorrow when you wake up, I want you to study yourself very closely.

See if you are aware of the habits you have and the impact these habits have on your life.

Notice any habits that hold you back. Do you give up when something seems too hard or keep quiet when you feel that you should speak up?

Habits are hard to break, but it is doable.

Once you know what needs to be improved or removed from your life, you can move in the direction of progressive change.

It took time for us to become who we are right now, and it will take more time to develop and grow. Still, it doesn't matter how long it takes—it only matters that we get there.

Make a list of the habits you wish to strengthen and then, in another column, a list of the habits that no longer serve you.

Choose one item from each column and make these two habits your focus for the next month. After each one, write a few sentences about the change that you will see in your life because of your success and perseverance.

Each morning in the month ahead, spend a moment envisioning this positive change. Each evening, think about how successful you were at strengthening your positive habit and leaving behind the habit that no longer serves you. If you don't make the progress you expect, ask yourself what is holding you back and how you can overcome that barrier.

At the end of the month, start again, choosing two more habits to focus on. Whatever progress you've made (or haven't made) on the first two habits, put them aside for now. Start anew. What's most critical is that you learn more about what motivates you and what challenges you. With that new awareness, you can continue to adjust your direction to align with your vision for your life.

The good thing about love is that it endures all things. Find comfort in knowing that whatever your hardships are in life, even when you run into a self-made barrier, your love and devotion to yourself is more than enough to overcome it.

Awareness Mantra

I'm aware of who I am.

I'm aware of who I am not.

If who I am is not who I want to be,

If who I am is not all that I am destined to be,

I'm aware that by looking within,

I shall find all that I've been searching for.

I'm aware that I am so much more than my doubts.

———————

Love what you see
inside of you because
it's a part of you, and
all of you is
beautiful.

IV.
FAITH

If I told you that I knew of a distant land where the sun was blue and the sky was orange, would you believe me? There, the grass grows purple and the tulips blossom from the trees.

My goddaughter asked me where there is such a place.

"In your mind," I responded. "If you take life one step at a time and have faith, there is nothing you can't find inside of you."

Faith is belief in things hoped for, without evidence.
As I grew up, people in our church would often say, "You must have faith."

"If you have faith, there is nothing that you can't survive."

While those beliefs still hold true for me, I've evolved to see faith in a new way, too.

It can't be argued: faith is invaluable to survival.

Faith is the last line of defense for self-love.

Now, it's reasonable to plan according to your ability. Part of strategizing is making sure that your goals are achievable.

Naturally, you may ask, "Well, how do I know that something can be achieved if I don't have evidence of my ability to accomplish it?"

This perspective is valid. It's a fine line between being confident—trusting that something can be achieved—and having faith.

Trust and faith each have their place in our journey and serve their own purpose. Although the two words are sometimes used interchangeably, they are not the same.

Faith is more synonymous with hope and optimism. You can't know for sure that something will happen, but you must have faith to even begin, and to then stay on course.

Trust is based on evidence and reason.

Faith holds your heart when trust can no longer hold your hand.

Let me give you an example, because this is important.

There was a father who thought it would be a good idea to take his son camping and spend the night under the stars. His son is terrified of being in the woods at night, but the trust he has in his father outweighs his fear. He knows his dad has been camping many times before. They pack their equipment and head out. Escaping into the country beyond their mid-sized town, they finally park and head into the deep woods. It's now dark. Their path is beneath the trees, hidden even from the night sky above.

The boy is anxious, but he trusts his father. He knows that if he has his dad, everything will be okay.

Finally, they stop and set up camp, putting up their tent and organizing their supplies to make sure that they have everything they could need.

Just as expected, the dad didn't forget anything. He was thorough as usual. The boy thinks to himself, "That's why I trust my dad. He never lets me down."

The trust the boy has in his father's abilities is based on the evidence of his father's previous actions.

Let's replay this scenario, except that the father has no previous camping experience. The boy is scared and maybe his dad is too.

The son can't trust his dad to know how to prepare for camping, but he can have faith. Faith tells him that his dad has been trustworthy in everything they've done together to this point, and even when things haven't turned out the way they wanted, his dad found a way through.

The dad has faith that, whatever comes up, they'll be able to adjust and adapt.

Without faith, they wouldn't venture into the unknown. That would be terrible, because many of the most precious moments in life are found where we least expect to find them.

Faith is a critical element in self-love because you can never be entirely certain how things will turn out. You don't know that this time, or even the 10th time, will work. But you try anyway.

If trust is damaged, it must be rebuilt from the foundation. But faith is resilient. You can have faith in someone's ability to grow even if your trust in them has been damaged by a serious mistake they've made. This is true of yourself, as well.

When I was studying to become a financial adviser, I had faith that I would pass all my tests the first time. It didn't happen that way.

I could have been so disappointed in myself that I spiraled into self-doubt and depression. I could have given up. But there was something inside of me that wouldn't let me quit. I couldn't bear the thought of it! Failure was not an option and there was a burning sensation in my gut telling me that I would get through it. I finally did.

That burning sensation was faith.

Years ago, my friend Toya made a bold move to take control of her happiness. With faith in herself, she moved from Texas to Dubai after losing her father to cancer and breaking up with her boyfriend.

While in Dubai, things became easier and she started to make progress. Life was going great for her. She grew accustomed to the culture, refocused on her vision for her life and was soon dating again.

But after two years in Dubai, the relationship she'd built there came to an end. Once again, she felt broken.

This time, she completely lost her faith in finding happiness. She asked me what I thought she should do, go to Vietnam and Cambodia for a holiday to celebrate her birthday, or return home.

I encouraged her to ask her heart that question.

"Which option do you believe will restore your faith in relationships with people?" I asked her. "And why?"

She thought about it for a while and chose to return home to be around the people she loves. She reconnected with friends and family. The experiences and expressions of love that she thought she'd lost returned to her.

When she returned to her job in Dubai, she was renewed. The genuine love she had for herself was revived when she reconnected with those who reminded her of who she was.

When battling addiction, problems in your job or in your relationship, you can't always be certain of the outcome. But having faith and being positive can go a long way. Faith keeps you and secures you when trust can no longer assure you.

No one knows with absolute certainty if their decisions are truly best for them. Neither can anyone be 100 percent confident that their actions will make them happy. But we will *never* know if we don't have faith and try.

There will be many times in every life when faith is so much more important than trust and confidence. In fact, it is faith that allows us to build trust and confidence.

When failure and rejection cripple trust and confidence, as they will, you will find your faith is refueled by an unwavering commitment to yourself and whatever you hold dear.

If you truly want to love yourself through all pain and disappointment, then you must believe that everything will work out for the better.

Now let's go back to the father and son in the woods. As the two venture out into the woods, tearing through branches and tripping over roots, the dad suddenly drops to his knees, clenching his jaws in obvious agony. He grabs for his phone and holds it up, trying to get a signal.

Frightened, the son asks what's wrong.

"I think it's my heart, son," the dad manages to say through his pain. "Run to the campsite and get help. Take my phone—look for a signal."

The boy panics. He knows nothing about the outdoors. How can he find a campsite in the dark?

But he doesn't have a choice.

Where he has no confidence or trust in himself, faith steps in.

The boy runs, still stumbling over roots, still terrified. He makes a few wrong turns, even losing the trail, but he knows that he can't quit. He calms himself, retraces his steps and finds his way back.

Finally, he sees a light ahead. He finds another camper who knows where to find a cell signal, and they call for an ambulance.

The boy saves his father. His faith has taken him where trust could not.

A woman wants to change jobs because she is no longer happy. She feels depressed and hates her life. She is slowly becoming an angry, impatient person. Her family is hurting because she can't help taking her unhappiness out on them.

One day at a time, she is losing herself. She is losing her family. She knows that if she stays in this job, she will eventually lose everything. She can't be confident in what lays ahead, but she knows that she must have faith.

Faith is the willingness to take risks to reach your goals and find happiness. If happiness is not present where you are, faith allows you to go find it elsewhere.

I too have had to make tough decisions in my life. There have been times when my friends have said that I'd changed, or my mother has called me distant. My sister, always honest, even said that she didn't recognize me anymore. The love I had for myself had been depleted, my happiness along with it. There was no way I could know for sure that everything would be okay, but I knew that I wouldn't last much longer if I didn't do something.

I felt like a complete outcast joining the military at almost 22, but while in bootcamp, I became dorm chief, the student leader in charge of my flight of 60 airmen.

After bootcamp, we moved on to advanced technical school. I had such culture shock being around so many people with different tastes, people who loved country music and movies I'd never heard of. They taught me and I taught them, but it was clear I was in a completely new world.

My high school was diverse, and I hung out with everyone; but when I went home, it was just my culture. In advanced technical school, it was 24/7 immersion in different cultures, and I learned so much. It is why I'm a firm believer in hanging out with people who are not like you, and traveling to understand how people in other places look at life.

I have friends that have never been outside of Dallas. Being in the military taught me that you have to leave home to understand yourself, other people and life. It opens your mind to so many different ideas: How you can make money, how you can be a good person, and how you can receive everything good in life.

After service in Portugal, I moved to England. I was having a great time, excelling at work. I was deployed to Qatar to serve my country.

After my deployment, I went back to England and met a beautiful woman. I was 25 years old. Then and to this day, she is the only woman I've ever said I love you to.

She came to America with me after I left the forces, getting her own apartment because we both wanted to do everything the right way.

A few years later, the relationship ended, shattering us both. I was sabotaging my happiness; I was sabotaging her happiness.

We broke up, and for about 10 months, I just stayed in my apartment.

I didn't even cry. I just thought about how I was once again at my lowest point in life.

I lost 20 pounds, my hair grew long, and my savings diminished. Finally, after 10 months of deep grief and depression, I forced myself to start opening my blinds to let some sunlight in. That small action finally led to confiding in my friends. Once I did, I couldn't stop.

As my healing progressed, I went back to studying to be a financial advisor. It was so hard to study because every single word I read made me think of my ex. But I finally passed my test, and that achievement also helped to lift me out of my depression.

I had stepped out in faith and gone where trust couldn't take me.

Experiencing severe depression twice in my life means that I know firsthand how bad things can get. I also know that it is possible to recover. With that experience, I can confidently encourage others to take similar leaps of faith.

Commit to yourself. It's time to do whatever it is that will make you happy.

The further I stepped out in faith, and with each situation I survived, the stronger my confidence grew.

Faith eventually led me to a place where I was able to trust myself because I'd proven my abilities.

It was then that I learned to love myself wholeheartedly.

I was better than the old Mike. I had become a man that I didn't even know I had the potential to be.

I had become myself.

While trust and confidence are important, they are limited to what has been proven in the past. Our futures are not certain, and you will need faith to take you to places you have never been before.

As you build upon your self-love, remember: Confidence and trust lead you to the river, but faith gets you across.

Your Action Item

Think of three things you want to do within the next year that require faith.

Do not worry about having the money, time, skills or support to do these things. This will be an ongoing experiment, exercising your faith, building confidence and gathering resources along the way.

Take a few moments and visualize yourself there, in that moment of achievement. Maybe you want to write a book or start a new job. Picture yourself at a book signing or in your new office—wherever you will feel as if you've made it. Experience the fulfillment.

Write these three things down.

Now, every week, I want you to record one thing that you have done to move towards your goals.

As time goes on, uncertainty will turn into certainty. Hope will evolve into confidence with each small task you accomplish.

Hold onto your faith. Let it be your eyes and guide your footsteps.

I look forward to seeing you on the other side, a stronger and bolder you, radiating self-love.

Faith Mantra

I walk by faith.

Not by sight.

Seeing only what frees me.

Letting go of what binds me.

Humans see with their eyes.

God sees with the heart.

Because of love, I commit to my path.

By faith, I shall never part from it.

_____

A situation may expose
who you are **in that
moment,** but it does
not define who you are
**at the center of
your soul.**

SECTION ONE

Things to Remember

+ Self-love is more than your soul's anchor—it's your own North Star. Your desires spring from your heart; pleasing yourself is the gateway to your happiness.

+ As you grow in self-love, you will develop the gift of discernment and gain access to a new mindset. You will eventually understand that all you can do in this world is be yourself.

+ We are human beings first, each of us searching for ways to improve our lives and ourselves. Examining your own life, analyzing the things you do and say, are necessary components of self-reflection. Who do you want to be while you are living?

+ Once we have become aware of the emotions, thoughts, beliefs and habits that drive our actions, progressive change is inevitable.

+ While trust and confidence are important, they are limited to what has been proven in the past. Our futures are not certain, and we need faith to take us to places we have never been. As you build upon your self-love, remember that confidence and trust lead you to the river, but faith gets you across.

PART TWO

Giving Yourself that Good, Good Love

I

BEING HONEST WITH YOU

To thine own self be true!

I used to say these words from Shakespeare's Hamlet to someone I really cared about, a woman who had moments when she just couldn't see the best in herself.

I've always believed that you won't have anything to give anyone else if you don't fill yourself up first. If we can't love ourselves, the love we try to give others will be tangled in our own unmet needs and insecurities.

So how do we see the best in ourselves? How do we fill ourselves up with love that then spills effortlessly onto the people in our lives?

Believe it or not, the next step in the process is self-honesty.

The truth is that most of our lives are already full and running over—but they are full of other people's business, other people's expectations, other people's values, other people's idea of success, other people's judgements. Self-honesty allows us to gradually let go of all that, filling our lives with whatever it is that makes us happy.

There are several different ways that we can practice being honest with ourselves. We will get there, but first let's talk about what being honest with yourself is and why it's so critical.

You might be thinking, but wait, Mike, I am always honest with myself. When I pass by the aisle with all the snacks that aren't good for me, I keep pushing my cart full speed ahead. I'm honest with myself about not being able to resist junk food once it's in my home.

Excellent. Most of the time, I do the same because I am very health conscious for my own reasons.

But self-honesty is also about knowing *why* you choose to do what you are doing. Why are you able to apply self-discipline in this situation and not in others? What is motivating you to eat healthy food?

Having this depth of understanding about ourselves is a kind of superpower, because it means we can then create systems that support us in achieving everything we want.

Self-honesty is doing what you do because you have done your research and understand the logic and emotion behind your decisions.

Are you clear about your reasons for dashing by the potato chip aisle? Is this level of self-discipline something you want for future you? Or are you depriving yourself of a pleasurable treat because someone else has made you feel ashamed?

"Don't eat that, you will gain weight." (As if gaining weight is the worst thing that could happen to you!)

"Don't you care about your health?!" (As if an occasional treat isn't part of a big beautiful healthy life!)

Just as we should not judge others or the way they choose to live their lives, we have to apply discernment when someone tells us how to live ours.

Sometimes we want to be in amazing shape so that we feel our best for a special event or because it makes us feel great and aligns with our lifestyle. Other people don't mind a few extra pounds. They figure they only have one life and they should enjoy it as much as possible, and that means delectable food. They do what pleases them and I also love that ideology.

It's your life—do what puts a smile on your face!

So, do you know what puts a smile on your face? Do you know how to make more room for those things in your life?

Self-honesty gives you the ability to live your life the way you want to—and be excellent at it.

Loving the Beautiful Body
that Moves You

One of the main reasons I knew I needed to write this book was because three people I cared for came to me during some of the most difficult times of their lives and asked for my help. In all three of those situations, they were comparing themselves to an air-brushed media ideal of beauty and feeling inadequate. It wasn't a small thing—they felt depressed, anxious and unable to cope. They were filled with self-loathing. They'd internalized the advertising world's standard of "beauty," designed to make us feel bad so we have to buy things to fix ourselves.

For my beautiful friends, a steady diet of this toxic messaging led to their self-love deserting them.

It happens to all of us sometimes—our self-love momentarily can't be found. And let's face it, loving our bodies is one of the final frontiers of self-love.

There is a well-known scene on the Oprah Show when fitness celeb Bob Greene asked Oprah if anyone was telling her the truth about how she looked. His implication was that people weren't being honest with her, and if they were, she would do something about her weight. For millions of people watching the show, it was a shocking moment. You're talking to *Oprah*—and you have the nerve to suggest that her weight has something to do with how people feel about her? I mean, that may be true of some people, but if it is, that is their own sad issue, not Oprah's issue. This kind of "truth" is really a mass of judgement from people who have been brainwashed into seeing human beauty as a certain size, shape and level of muscle tone. It's a way of keeping us all from focusing on the things that really matter. It's a way to keep us from loving ourselves, the source of all our power.

The media can be so cruel. I once read an article that was titled, "Top 50: Most Beautiful Women in the World." None of the women were fully Black and only two were mixed. I was outraged.

Black women are gorgeous—I want them to know that. It is beyond time for media outlets to reflect that there are absolutely stunning people of all ethnicities. A bias for Caucasian features is simply a developmental delay caused by a limited worldview.

One of the most gorgeous women I ever met in my life didn't look anything like the media portrays as beautiful. That took nothing away from her beauty. Her personality was undeniably attractive, and her mind was alluring. She was stunning and confident.

She knew that, if you start changing who you are because someone tells you what you should or shouldn't do, you're not being faithful to yourself. If you're not being faithful to yourself, you're dimming the light that God gave you.

Nothing delights my heart more than seeing someone comfortable in the skin that God has blessed them with. Now that's beauty.

Right for Me? Or Just Right for You?

Please understand that I am not saying that others cannot give you advice worth listening to. My brothers and sisters keep me focused all the time and I do the same for them. No one can make it in this world on their own, without any guidance or assistance. However, when my brothers and sisters communicate their experience and knowledge, I don't agree with them simply for the sake of doing so. Instead, I take their perspective into consideration and analyze how it aligns with my lifestyle. Whatever I find beneficial and applicable to my situation, I adopt for myself.

It's not disrespect for their views that stops me from integrating everything that works for them into my own life. It is just that what is relevant to them may not be relevant to my life and personal development.

What I am saying is that no one's thinking strategy is absolute. Their worlds are different than my own and I must play by the rules that best complement my journey.

This is what being honest with yourself is about: seeing things as they really are, accepting your truth, clarifying your moral compass and making your own decisions to improve your life.

It is seeing yourself without excuses and being honest about what helps or hurts you.

Practicing Self-Honesty
in Relationships

It sounds simple, right? But it is human nature to make excuses for ourselves about the things we do. It takes self-love and confidence to own our stuff instead of trying to shift it onto someone else.

For example, let's say you're frustrated with your partner. He is just on your nerves. Now you come home for dinner after work and there is a burnt pizza smoking in the oven while he plays video games in the living room. You lose it, raising your voice, telling him he doesn't support you or care about you.

Or you might just storm out and come home five hours later. Yes, we have surely all been there.

Being honest with yourself means knowing there is an underlying reason for everything you do.

In this case, it's helpful to ask why we are so close to our edge. What's going on in your life that is making you irritable? Do you need to have a serious think or even talk about the relationship? Or is your partner just where you're focusing your anger and anxiety right now?

Think your situation all the way through. If you were at your best, wouldn't you just laugh, hug your partner in sympathy and suggest take-out or cereal for dinner? Wouldn't that approach be a lot more likely to ensure a good night ahead (versus a likely month or so of cooking your own meals)?

So, if you know that, why might things go in a different direction? What is making you lose faith with yourself?

Perhaps you haven't been getting enough sleep or you're worried about money. Perhaps there are real problems in the relationship, but you've been avoiding a difficult conversation.

Whatever the underlying factors are, what matters most is self-honesty. Not being accountable for your role in any situation robs you of the opportunity to move forward. Self-honesty is getting beyond your defensive ego and asking, "What am I feeling? Why am I feeling this way? Are my feelings alerting me to something I need to change?"

Once you are honest with yourself, you have the power to make real, lasting change. In your relationships, elevating to a state of honesty with yourself will also give you the ability to see beyond the masks other people often wear. You'll begin to look for and see the underlying factors that make them do what they do, too.

Need a Hand? Everybody Does Sometime

Self-honesty won't happen instantly. And it probably won't be your default position 100 percent of the time, no matter how long you practice it.

Much of what we see is based on someone else's influence. From birth, we identify with the family we were born into and with friends whose lives closely resemble our own. We are raised by our mothers and fathers, sometimes by grandparents or other relatives. We share physical features and behavioral traits.

These people greatly influence our development. Our morals, values and principles are usually based on what we experience and are taught. It's only natural that those closest to us have the greatest impact on who we are.

This can be a wonderful thing. But it is likely to leave you with some unhelpful ideas and behaviors, too. Acknowledging your family dynamics and those of the friends closest to you allows you to start to see any toxic behavior that may be present in your life.

If you are honest about which of these leftover ideas and behaviors aren't serving you, you have an opportunity to progress over time by replacing them with more effective approaches.

We will run into obstacles. Sadly, it is more common than not to experience trauma, as children or later in life. That means that most of us will be in need of some kind of emotional assistance at some point. It is pivotal to understand that we are not victims of our circumstances, without any source of relief. Sometimes we need help and that's okay. Being honest enough to admit that we can't do it on our own is a major step toward growth.

If that is where you find yourself today, congratulations on reaching this milestone. You are a champion already because you are taking control of your situation and evolving.

Occasionally we just hit random roadblocks. When this happens to you, I encourage you to see and embrace your reality—but don't accept it as your destiny.

In my heart, I know we all can evolve out of any condition we are subjected to. I've done it myself and I have all the faith in the world that your desires can take you anywhere your heart is willing to follow.

When you love yourself, your work ethic exceeds your aspirations—and your heart and life fill with joy.

Self-Honesty and Communication

As much as we are inclined to at times, we can't control other people's actions. (Morally speaking, we shouldn't want to, but there are times when that desire reveals itself.) However, we do have autonomy over what we tolerate. As hard as it may be, do your best not to make excuses for others' behavior.

"Oh, she didn't mean it."

"He was just joking around."

"They are having a rough time."

These are excuses we routinely fabricate for others when we don't have the strength to see people for who they truly are. It amazes me how, when we create a space for growth between us and those who don't contribute to our success, we're able to see clearer. Distance becomes a correspondent of truth that directs us towards a greater version of ourselves.

People will always be who they are and there is nothing we can do about that. It's only natural not to want to see anything negative in those we love and respect. Having to accept this kind of truth is never comfortable.

In any relationship I've had, I've been fortunate to leave the situation as a more mature and enlightened person than I was when it began. Spending intimate time with someone exposes new truths.

Loving relationships can stir up things within us like nothing else. We permit those we love to access parts of our lives that are off limits to anyone else. This may be true of moments of our pasts too sensitive for even us to go near, which is why we try to forget them.

There's a level of vulnerability that can be terrifying because we can never be certain of anyone else's intentions. Every facet of our life becomes intertwined with that special someone.

For all these reasons, a relationship rooted in effective communication and mutual respect can produce some of the most amazing moments of our lives. Likewise, relationships can provoke some of our most shattering experiences as well.

Life is a balance of highs and lows, and our relationships are not exempt from this universal law. But honesty between you and your partner can help prevent many of the worst problems. In any important relationship, our aim is happiness. We want blissful thoughts when we even *think* about our intimate relationship. The only way I have found to accomplish this is to build the relationship on respectful, honest conversations.

One of my favorite examples of how honesty can secure a healthy relationship comes from a fellow patriot I proudly served with. Thinking about Jimenez and the passionate way he loves his wife still puts a smile on my face. They have been together since they were 15 and have the most amazing relationship. To find each other at a young age and grow in love for over two decades is remarkable.

I found it so inspiring to witness such loving energy between two people. Being the person I am, always in pursuit of knowledge, I couldn't help but ask Jimenez how they maintain such an extraordinary connection. In fact, I asked him a number of times, because I had a hard time believing it was as simple as he made it out to be.

He always gave me the same answer.

"Honesty and communication. You get to know who your partner is and who they are not, inside and out."

He went on to explain that, with honesty, you can know each other fully and make decisions that manifest love and patience. You can motivate and be strong for each other, providing support when your partner can't be strong for themselves.

Anything can happen at any time, Jimenez said, but if you are honest with each other, you can overcome whatever comes your way.

"Be honest and willing to communicate—and the rest will take care of itself."

My ex and I had an incredibly intimate conversation years after our relationship had ended. She was being so honest about such a hard topic.

"I was in love with you," I told her. "I wanted to give you all of my energy when you were going through that time. I wanted to be the person you went through it with, so that you didn't have to go through it by yourself."

My heart aches knowing I made that time harder for her. I wasn't yet self-honest enough to know that I was trying to fix things that could only be grieved.

Once I really understood Jimenez' blueprint, I didn't waste any time applying it to all things in my life. As a financial adviser, it allowed me to help my clients manifest their dreams by making educated decisions.

"So, how about we try being honest with ourselves and asking what is affordable for your life? Can you afford your lifestyle without the means to sustain it?" Just because you have the money in your account doesn't mean you can spend it.

We can apply this logic to our dating decisions as well. Your single status doesn't mean you can emotionally afford to invest yourself in another person—it may be more beneficial to invest that time in yourself.

How many of us have jumped into relationships way before we were ready? We saw ourselves hurting but were not honest about the depth of our pain. So, we figure this person will be different than the one before and make everything okay. Then to our surprise, it happens again. Another relationship has failed, and it validates what we believed to be the problem the entire time: Everyone but us.

Everyone's the same, right?!

I am done with men!

I am done with women!

There is an old saying that goes, "Point one finger at someone else and you have three pointing back at you."

We all play our part in any human interaction. Be willing to open up and explore the possibility that there is something you can do better.

Be honest about what you see when you look at your life and then move on to the next step, acceptance.

Love what you see inside of yourself because it's a part of you, and all of you is beautiful. What lies within us is valuable; we should be the one who cherishes it the most.

So many treasured materials are found buried in another substance. Diamonds, gold and oil are all hidden from sight, deep in the Earth. We too have something precious buried deep within us.

Be honest about who you are. See the truth within and want it. Don't go a single day without telling yourself how much you love yourself and how awesome you are. Celebrate you. Wear your favorite rain boots under your brightly colored umbrella on the sunniest day if you want. Who cares, if you are happy, smiling and laughing when you do it?

Losing Yourself, Finding Yourself

It really hurts my heart when I see how many people are unhappy because they've allowed someone to tap into their self-love and disrupt their signal. I've lost count of how many people I have met who don't like where they are in life or even who they are as a person. When I've asked them what happened, the most common response is that they were trying to make someone else happy.

It is easy to lose sight of ourselves when looking through the lens of someone else's ambitions and interests. Prioritizing someone else's needs can become an obsession, an endless need to define yourself by your reflection in their eyes.

We rarely stop to inquire about that person's allegiance to our development. How has their involvement in our life contributed to our growth as a person?

We can accomplish many things in life. But very few things feel as rewarding as becoming a better human—a better us—as defined by our own heart. When we put the needs of others before our own, that is what we're sacrificing.

This was something that another friend of mine learned the hard way. As she desperately tried to save others, she was the one truly suffering, and there was no one to save her.

Eventually she realized she felt empty and alone. She became determined to have a child. She tried to conceive, only to have months and then years pass without a pregnancy. She was heartbroken and felt like a complete failure. So many times before, she felt she had fallen short—now she was unable to do the thing she'd believed her body was naturally designed to do.

She struggled for a while, but she eventually came to believe that her inability to conceive was God telling her that she was not yet ready to be a mother. In response to this spiritual awakening, she decided to write a list of commitments that she would hold herself to in respect to her unborn child.

It wasn't the easiest thing to do, despite how motivated she was. She didn't know what made her happy because she didn't know herself. Her life had been dedicated to others. She couldn't succeed at something that she didn't understand.

It took time, but by remaining committed to loving herself a little more, day by day, she began to discover who she was. Over time, she began to not only love who she was, but to long for herself and for her own company and truth.

She found love, peace and joy in places that were once dark. Her life was now the brightest star in the universe.

She knew she was ready to be a mom. But she also knew that the child she had been longing for was no longer required to complete her or her life.

She was enough.

Your Action Item

Creating happiness in your life takes time, patience and courage.

We are going to practice making a mental note of small opportunities that life presents to please ourselves.

This activity has three parts.

First, I want you to go about your day and just pay attention to those moments when someone else's focus is on you. As soon as you can afterward, make a quick note to yourself on your phone or a piece of paper.

Pay attention to glances that seem approving or disapproving, to every time someone says something to you like, "Why did you do that? You should ..."

After about a week of this practice, find a quiet place and take some time for yourself. Start by sitting in silence for five minutes. Clear your mind and relax your body.

Now, take out your notes and look at all the times over the week that someone had something to say about you.

Think about how you felt in that moment and how you responded. Observe how many times you changed your thinking or actions because of someone else's discomfort.

How much of your energy did you spend pleasing others? How many times did you deny yourself in order to comfort another person's ego or insecurity?

Don't feel bad or judge yourself. It happened. These are the experiences that help build us into stronger people, capable of greater things. Accept your responses and actions without making any excuses.

Now, think about how you wish you had responded. What do you wish you would've said or done, if anything, at the time?

Examine your heart and mind. What held you back from being yourself?

Be unsparingly honest when writing your responses. Once again, don't fall into the very human tendency to look for others to blame for your feelings or actions. They have their own deal—this is about you, for your benefit.

When you finish reflecting on these experiences and the ways you'd like to respond in similar situations going forward, put these notes away.

This week is done, and tomorrow is a new day. Bear in mind that yard by yard, things may seem extremely difficult—but inch by inch, all things are possible. Any one situation may shed light on who you were in that moment, but it does not define who you are.

Be bold and daring. Embrace the opportunity to be a truer version of you, tomorrow and every day ahead.

I challenge you to rise, like the phoenix that rises from the ashes of its own burnt body. Cast off any negative feelings from this exercise. Take only the beautiful, living lessons with you.

A scripture that keeps me encouraged when I fall short is 2 Corinthians 4:7-9.

But we have this treasure in jars of clay to show that this all-surpassing power is from God and not from us. We are hard pressed on every side, but not crushed; perplexed, but not in despair; persecuted, but not abandoned; struck down but not destroyed.

Despite what you may believe about your situation today, you are too blessed to be stressed.

Honesty Mantra

Honesty is bold.

To see myself is brave.

And to forgive is courageous.

This is the life I choose to live.

Loving from within.

Embracing my insecurities.

Owning my faults.

All of me is what I love.

—————

Being honest with yourself illuminates your path to **emotional freedom,** and acceptance **sets you free.**

II.
ACCEPTANCE

"Life is a series of natural and spontaneous changes. Don't resist them; that only creates sorrow. Let reality be reality. Let things flow naturally forward in whatever way they like."

LAO TZU

We've already accomplished a lot and grown in ways that will bless us all, and the world around us, throughout our lifetimes. Ultimately, that's what life and love are about—knowledge, understanding and growth.

I'm overjoyed to have you on this journey with me.

While we've covered much ground, we're not all the way there yet.

Our next step is working toward accepting what we've discovered, so we can begin to heal.

Being honest about what we feel inside, who we are as people and the influences that impact our lives are all vital fundamentals of self-love. But it's not enough to be a witness to ourselves and the world. We must accept ourselves as we are and then work relentlessly toward our full potential. We must accept the world as it is, and then work relentlessly to change it for the better.

Most of us were raised in some sort of shame tradition— that is, the adults around us had been taught that the best way to make us do better was to make us ashamed when we did something wrong. But we now know the opposite is true. Guilt and shame are not synonymous—when we feel guilty, we know we have missed the mark and need to do better in the future. When we feel shame, we feel that we are hopeless and that, no matter how hard we try, we are unworthy of love. Guilt can be motivating, but shame is paralyzing. Shame triggers our ego, which then tries to protect us from change through defensiveness, fear and anger.

With self-love, we can begin to exorcise the shame we've collected throughout our lives—to cast off any belief that we aren't capable of contributing great things to the world around us.

There are countless people living in denial about things that happened in their pasts. They're unwilling to accept that their experiences were real and had consequences. Whether they know it or not, they are living in shame and ego. Instead of being able to incorporate the lessons of their experiences and move on, they get stuck.

This is what the wise ones mean when they say, "Wherever you go, there you are."

Keeping those experiences of disappointment and shame

locked away doesn't change their existence. Whatever reason a person has for being unable to confront their truths, the crippling effect of unacknowledged experiences is still present. It doesn't go away because they're unwilling to acknowledge it.

Being honest with yourself illuminates your path so that you can see clearly. But only acceptance sets you free to embrace your vision for your life and start working towards freedom.

Galileo, known as the founder of observational astronomy, modern science, physics and the scientific method, said, "All truths are easy to comprehend once they are discovered; the point is to discover them."

Loving yourself the way you deserve to be loved is not the most complicated thing to do, but the importance of doing so can be a hard truth to discover. Some people believe they are not worth loving.

Last year I received a letter from Joslin, who lived in Maine and was in her mid-20s at the time. She wrote to me about a toxic relationship she'd been in and her struggle to pick up the pieces afterward.

She wanted help with accepting what had happened and moving forward. Joslin wanted nothing more than to regain control of her life and be happy again.

She and her former partner Justin were from the same hometown and he'd recently returned after being discharged from the Army. Initially, their reunion was delightful. They enjoyed every moment of each other's company.

It wasn't long, though, before the fairy tale reunion ended

abruptly. He struggled with horrific events that happened during his military service and with Post-Traumatic Stress Disorder. He was unable to accept things he had done in service to his country, and he began trying to cope with alcohol and drugs. It soon spiraled into what seemed like an irreversible addiction. His behavior became erratic and aggressive.

Joslin became insecure and stopped seeing the wonderful person she is. Even though she knew Justin was troubled, she began to believe in his view of her.

When their relationship became unbearable, she broke up with him. It was a wake-up call for him, and he stopped drinking and doing drugs. They reconnected. But it wasn't long before the weight of his PTSD would prove too great. Once again, he was soon smoking and drinking, starting at the beginning of the day. His behavior and decision-making were far worse than before.

This was very difficult for Joslin to accept because she wanted more out of life.

Then she was accepted by a medical school in Florida. It should have been incredible news for them both, but Justin was negative about her accomplishment because he felt the school was too far away.

He was scared to leave home again. She could no longer stay.

Justin broke up with Joslin on Valentine's Day and it shattered her. He resented her for wanting more in life than he did. She cried for four days straight and was unable to eat.

Her inability to accept who Justin was and the incompatibility of their visions for their lives cost her dearly. Even more destructive was her inability to accept that she deserved more, that she was worth more than a life she didn't want.

Joslin's story is so common. How many of us have been in a similar situation at some point, whether it's a relationship or a job that isn't right for us?

It's not enough to see; we must see clearly. Even when it feels like other people are the source of our challenges, the change must begin within us.

Acceptance is not just seeing with your eyes but acknowledging and accepting your reality with your mind and heart. When Joslin realized that she couldn't change Justin and accepted him for who he really was, they both understood their relationship had to end.

It's always easier to identify other people's problems. We aren't as adept at spotting our own, but by giving ourselves time to reflect, with self-honesty, we can begin to see the blind spots and excuses that hinder our growth.

Focusing on how you can improve your life is a proactive approach to change. Give yourself permission to accept that you can improve, and that you currently have some habits or patterns that aren't serving you well.

Also, try not to compare yourself to others. Remember that people put their best moments on Instagram; comparing them to your ordinary moments can be so damaging to your vision of yourself.

In an interview before his death, the rapper Mac Miller

described our interactions with social media perfectly: "We fear rejection, want attention, crave affection, and dream of perfection."

How many of us wake up and scroll through our feeds before we even roll out of bed?

We see someone we admire and tell ourselves, okay, I need to be like that person.

No, you do not. The person you need to be is the one looking at you in the mirror.

You are capable of much more than you give yourself credit for. I would like to think there is a reason that no two fingerprints are the same. God didn't create us to hold someone else's dreams in our hands. You have your own unique ambitions, gifts and vision. Focus there.

2 Timothy 1:7 says, "For God has not given us a spirit of fear, but of power and of love and of a sound mind." It doesn't matter if you don't have her physique; she doesn't have your smile and your smile is luminous. It doesn't matter that you don't have his muscle tone; he doesn't have your charisma and engaging personality. While you are looking at someone else's life, understand they are most likely doing the same thing.

Despite what many would have us believe, life is not a competition. As Emily Dickinson wrote, "Find ecstasy in life; the mere sense of living is joy enough."

Searching for your reflection in someone else's mirror is not accepting who you are. Don't compare yourself to others—you cannot be duplicated.

The artist Henri Matisse said, "He who loves, flies, runs and rejoices; he is free, and nothing holds him back." We know that isn't always true of the state that we call love in relationships. But true self-love is everything Matisse describes.

Be honest, accept yourself and love yourself.

Your Action Item

Let's do another exercise. This one will help us practice accepting our truth.

I want you to create a one-page journal entry about accepting yourself. Start by spending some time thinking about yourself as you are right now.

What have you noticed about yourself that you would like to change or improve? What do you find hardest to accept about yourself?

Is there some physical feature that you are self-conscious about? Okay, is this a problem? If so, for who? Is this someone for whom you would be willing to give yourself up for? If not, can you allow yourself to accept and love this God-given body exactly as it is?

What about your past? Is there something that happened to you or that you did that makes you feel physically uncomfortable each time it comes up in your mind? Think about your younger self with love and offer up some healing grace. Whatever happened, you were doing the best you could with what you knew at the time. You have survived everything you've gone through and learned so much along the way. Every one of those moments brought you here, where you are now fully equipped to create your own beautiful, completely unique future.

Now turn the page over. For each of the qualities, characteristics or events you wish you could change, write a few sentences of gratitude.

See yourself through the eyes of love. You'll know when you are, because when you do, you'll see that everything about you is beautiful right now, even those things you are working to change.

Acceptance Mantra

It's not enough to know.

It's not enough to see.

Acceptance is clarity.

The vision beyond sight.

The stardust in my eyes.

I will walk in my divine light of self-love.

———————

What lies within us is **valuable and indeed desirable,** and the person who desires us the most **should be us.**

III.
JUST ONE WIN

"You gotta go hard, you gotta believe in yourself.

You gotta have a sense of humor to know that the bullshit is gonna happen, you can't be too serious about it or too emotional and fake when the bullshit happens.

You gotta just stick to the script, believe and have an overwhelming confidence.

Be your own biggest fan, your own biggest believer, and put it on your back and carry the weight."

NIPSEY HUSSLE, RAPPER AND ENTREPRENEUR ...
FOREVER MISSED

Wow, we have really peeled back some layers. We've examined difficult and intimate issues. I hope you can feel the love, because I sure do.

Be happy. This is your time. I applaud your bravery and admire your honesty. Seeing things as they are is tough. It takes an enormous amount of courage.

To grow together to this point, it was necessary to confront our insecurities. Let's take a moment and celebrate that growth. Let's acknowledge that, even though we still have some things to work on, we are all sensational, brave people. We deserve love and praise, especially from ourselves.

If there is a part of your mind arguing with this truth, perhaps it is because you're experiencing some growing pains right now. I hope you find solace in the fact that you are still in the race.

There is no doubt in my mind that we will get there together. As humans, we all suffer insecurities and personal trauma. That is true regardless of sex, religion race or cultural experience. When life has you down and the way the people you love are treating you hurts, keep moving forward. Self-love, power and growth rise from the ashes of hardships. Love yourself!

Even if you feel that no one else loves you, you love you. That's enough.

"Success consists of going from failure to failure without loss of enthusiasm," is a quote often attributed to Winston Churchill.

Whatever is going on for you, I encourage you to hold on

to your faith in who you are and what you can become. Holding onto faith in the face of failure *is* a victory. These small victories may appear insignificant in comparison to the big picture, but they are priceless. Every moment of our existence counts, and every aspect of who you are matters.

To wish to change what we've experienced is to fail to appreciate the resilience and strength of our warrior spirit.

And always remember—all you need is one win to put that smile back on your face.

Limits are illusions. I wanted to be reminded of that regularly, so a tattoo on my chest looks back at me from my mirror each day: *Limitless.*

There is no limit to what you can achieve. Let me make that perfectly clear. If you aren't convinced, read the stories of people who have achieved amazing things, people like Malala Yousafzai, Nelson Mandela and Nick Vujicic. The most remarkable thing about those who achieve true greatness is not that they are great, but that they were once completely ordinary. They start out just like you and me, but they never stop in their efforts to become their greatest selves.

The late motivational speaker Zig Ziglar said, "It's your attitude, not your aptitude, that will determine your altitude." It's something that is proven in the biography of every accomplished person. The one thing that all of these people have in common is that they kept on going, and eventually overcame or went around the obstacles they encountered.

If you are willing to put in the work and make the sacrifices, to persevere while accepting the losses that provide the necessary experience, you can do anything!

Let's look at this idea from a different angle for a moment. A person who's in the pursuit of something great must be willing to work harder than they ever imagined possible. When we desire a life that brings more blessings than we already have, we must be willing to make sacrifices that will test our commitment to our aspirations.

In those moments, when you find yourself rising to the mightiest challenges you've ever faced, step out in faith. Remember that you've built the strength you need right now by surviving each of the challenges you've faced to this point. Were you bullied in school? Have you lived through poverty? Injustice? Has your heart been broken? Have you made humiliating mistakes?

The strength that comes from surviving hardship can become our superpower when we're willing to bet on ourselves. Be brave enough to take a chance. Sure, it may not result in getting what you want at this moment. But your persistence will build on itself and grow in power. Putting yourself in a position where you can fail takes courage, because no one wins all the time in life.

Something my grandmother used to say to me has kept me grounded in good and bad times.

"Michael, to whom much is given, much is required."

As humans, we desire a better life, whatever that means to us. Without these desires, many of us wouldn't be inspired to grind as hard as we do. They get us out of bed on our most difficult days and during life's most trying times.

However, we must also be aware that what we want in life may require us to be a person we haven't yet evolved into. Like my friend who realized that she needed to become the kind of mother she wanted to be before she had a child, we have to put in the work first.

We are molded and developed over time through experiences that equip us with wisdom, integrity and resilience. All of our experiences are necessary, and I believe our trying times are the most critical when it comes to growth.

Yes, the good moments are memorable and beautiful; they restore us for the next set of challenges. But those moments in which we feel embarrassed, ashamed, flattened—as if we are failures? These are the moments in which we grow and evolve into something more.

Your Action Item

Write the following affirmations on notecards and stick them on your mirror.

Read these words aloud to yourself each morning, and again each time you need to hear it.

I love myself enough to do this for me.

I love myself enough to never waste another moment or another opportunity.

I will be successful at loving myself because I deserve my love.

IV

LIFE *IS* THE LITTLE THINGS

"Make it a habit to tell people thank you. To express your appreciation, sincerely and without the expectation of anything in return. Truly appreciate those around you, and you'll soon find many others around you. Truly appreciate life and you'll find that you have more of it."

RALPH MARTSON, AUTHOR OF THE DAILY MOTIVATOR

When you feel enthusiastic about what you are doing, other people can't help but respond to the positive energy radiating around you.

A sense of accomplishment often triggers ambition for more. It feels good to pursue new ambitions—but dwelling in a state of constant pursuit can also lead to feeling chronically unsatisfied.

Let me be clear. There is absolutely nothing wrong with

pursuing your goals, accomplishing them and then redirecting your energy toward more. However, sometimes it seems that, no matter what we achieve, our next thought is about the *next* achievement. We cannot find the joy in our moments of success, never mind in the daily life between them.

As soon as we've grasped what we have been working, grinding and hustling for, we exchange our satisfaction for another ambition. We want more. And then more. We don't take the time to celebrate what we've just accomplished.

We can also miss out on the process that makes us who we are. As we disassociate from everything that helped us mature, we are once again in danger of losing ourselves.

To live in self-love, it is essential to take the time to enjoy the small things, all the little pleasures of life and the minor steps forward.

Each victory in our life builds confidence and faith. These are the elements of success, the tides that keep propelling our ship onward. The world is our ocean and it's our human right to explore it.

Think of faith and self-love as your sail; think of your values, morals and principles as the compass that guides you. This is what it means to follow your heart.

Remember my grandmother's wisdom: to whom much is given, much is required. So, take the time to appreciate the precious moments within the process that earns you your degree or that new promotion with the corner office.

"Though we travel the world over to find the beautiful, we must carry it with us, or we find it not," said Ralph Waldo Emerson. It's not the destination that we should be after—the reward is the adventures we experience during our journey.

Life is simply an experiment. Embrace every experience. Consider this wisdom from Emerson's dear friend Henry David Thoreau: "Our truest life is when we are in our dreams awake."

Celebrating Our Gifts

Do you stop regularly to remember the time when what you have now is all you wanted? If not, the desire for more can become an unquenchable thirst.

A friend once told me about a woman he met on a business retreat. Let's call her Fatim to protect her privacy. For years, Fatim dreamt of being an actor. She was already the first to graduate from college in her family. At the age of 23, she was well on her way to becoming an amazing artist and a women's rights activist. Painting life was her gift, capturing the world around her with the most vibrant shades of orange, blue and eccentric shades of pink. Though Fatim's talents were undeniable, what she wanted most was to be admired by a world that she felt didn't understand or accept her. She knew her art gave hope to people lost in life's transitions, but she wanted more—she wanted to be adored by those who were already famous. What she had accomplished was not enough for her, because she felt as if she didn't measure up to those who live in front of the camera.

She gave up her art in pursuit of fame because she forgot something important. As described by one of the founders of John Hopkins Hospital, William Osler: "We are here to add what we can to life, not to get what we can from life."

As Fatim struggled to find her way, she often thought of her art and the happiness it brought. It bothered her that she was willing to trade it all to just be seen by an audience.

Eventually, Fatim didn't like who she had become in her quest to become famous. The love she had for herself had faded; she felt she'd faded along with it. Fame paled in comparison to a life of compassion and service for others. She found her way back to her art and to herself, using self-love as her path and her light.

I've accomplished a lot and I'm very grateful for every opportunity given to me. It's been more than I ever imagined. Still, having a family and being there for my children, building that tree house for them, is the ultimate diamond in the sky for me. Perhaps because I grew up in a house of love, a happy family is Heaven on Earth to me.

But that's my truth. It's up to you to discover your truth.

Whatever you do, remember that nothing is greater than love. As we go out into the world to pursue great things, we must do our best not to neglect those who have been our cornerstones.

When in Doubt, Serve Others

Whatever we do, wherever we aim, it won't mean much unless we're serving others. When I was in the military, I participated in several volunteer opportunities and learned that helping others keeps me grounded. It reminded me where I started from and made me grateful for how far I'd come. One of my friends who volunteered with me, Anthony, used to say, "Gratitude is not only the greatest of virtues, but the parent of all others." I honestly cannot count how many times we went on details together in the community. What I do remember is how it helped him become a believer in self-love and self-care.

Like me, my friend was doing well for himself career-wise. He was one of those men who felt that you create your own path and then watch people follow.

"You should never stop to think about what was, focus on what is," he'd say.

He believed you just push through, no matter what.

However, life has a way of humbling us all in its own time and way. When Anthony's wife left him for someone else, he began to experience emotions and doubts he'd never faced before. He had to learn to be confident again, which scared him because he couldn't remember a moment when he didn't think he could do something. But we can never take anything for granted. When his time came, it nearly destroyed him. He was so in love with his wife.

I asked Anthony to come with me to do some volunteer work to help get his mind off things. Initially, he was against it, but there is something about asking someone something 100 times that makes the 101st time seem like a good idea! We went to a kids' shelter and when he had seen the way some children live, without a family to care for them, he burst into tears.

He turned to me and said, "Mike, I will always be grateful for this moment."

It really changed him and helped him realize how much people need each other.

There is something about giving back to our communities that helps us remember the necessity of a healthy, functioning community of happy people. Not everyone comes into this world with equal opportunities, so it's vital that those who can give, do.

Anthony began to let go of the grief and disillusionment that weighed him down and started to focus on what he could do to help lift others up. He is a great man and I am so proud to have served with him.

Celebrating these kinds of accomplishments and contributions is such a loving, happy experience. It takes us back to the roots that gave rise to our ambitions. Appreciating these moments can also help us deepen our daily process of self-reflection, which improves our ability to perform in life overall.

Patience, Perseverance and Repetition

Imagine that one of your goals is to reach an extreme level of fitness. You go on YouTube and see a video of a person who looks amazingly fit. They're radiating positivity and self-love.

You say to yourself, "I want to be like that person. I want to feel so good about myself that what others might think doesn't bother me at all."

You want to be there in that space, and you can. You can absolutely do it, but it will not happen immediately.

What you don't see on YouTube are the thousands of small moments of repetition. The person you can see spent years moving toward and celebrating small accomplishments.

No, they didn't just wake up that way.

Neither will you. Confidence and self-love don't grow on trees in the backyard. Faith and repetition are key!

We progressively evolve into the person we want to be. So, don't be too hard on yourself about who you are not, or what you are unable to do now. Each time you attempt to do something, even if you fail, you gain something in return.

Every single repetition counts. It's impossible to skip forward to the millionth time.

You must experience every moment, and that's okay.

Napoleon said that the starting point of all achievement is desire. As long as you maintain your desire, your confidence will grow with each attempt. You will grow. Okay, so you have not reached your goal—but you are one day closer than you were yesterday.

Changing your perception of yourself and the world around you will unquestionably change you. As inventor Thomas Edison said about his efforts to create a lightbulb: "I have not failed 10,000 times. I've just found 10,000 ways that won't work." He appreciated and valued each attempt; each small measure of experience was key to his progress.

In all of our efforts, the development of character is the true reward. Over time, the small things add up to something greater. If we aren't appreciative and grateful for every experience we have along the way in our life journey, we're missing our blessings.

Finally, do not be dismayed by those who judge you. I strongly believe in the saying, "If you have no critics, you will have no success."

Your Action Item

This is an exercise I encourage you to start doing each evening before you go to bed.

Take out your journal and write down one thing you did today that moved you toward the life you're building. It could be as simple as making your bed or as momentous as applying to college.

Now, write down the last thing you did that made someone else smile, an act of kindness or appreciation. Think about how you felt in that moment, about how you also benefited from that act of service.

Think about the last time someone offered you an act of service, even if it was just a warm, unexpected smile. Send out a prayer of gratitude and well-being to that person.

Finally, at the top of the page, write the date and the title:

Celebrations!

Sweet dreams.

Don't Forget the Little Things Mantra

A journey of a thousand miles begins with a single step.

Every inch becomes a foot, every foot grows into a mile.

Contributing to a cause greater than itself.

My life, masked in years, is a universe of small moments.

I will open the door to my heart and live.

———————

There is

never

a reason

anyone

should feel

less than

what they

are.

V.

WHEN YOU LEAP THE FENCE AND THE GRASS ISN'T GREENER

In this last chapter, I want to bring everything back full circle.

We have discussed what self-love is and the various ways we can incorporate it into our life. I know there are many of you out there who are now eager to just get on with the work.

However, I want you to take a moment and reflect on something.

There is a chance that after reaching your goals, you may find that they don't bring you the joy you had hoped for.

Henry David Thoreau left us with another idea that is applicable here: "It's not what you look at that matters, it's what you see."

We may experience a desire so intense that we are willing to do anything to achieve it. However, we may later discover that the outcome isn't quite what we imagined it would be.

In the end, there's no way to predict who we will be when we finally arrive on the shores of our ambitions. Things change; we change along with them. Always be prepared for a different you to appear. Be open-minded and willing to embrace a new course in life.

The grass may not be greener on the other side of our dreams, but it doesn't mean that the view can't still be beautiful.

Know that change is good. It is the most reliable constant in the universe. People who are unwilling to change and adapt to life will find themselves constantly lost in it. The one thing we absolutely cannot do is stay in a state of nostalgia and go nowhere. It isn't possible. Life is movement.

Having the choice to create love and manifest greatness is a true gift from the universe. You were born to be a gravitational force of positive change and hope. Life at this moment may not be what we want it to be, but now is always the starting point.

Be flexible in your approach to loving yourself and your life.

You already have everything on the inside that you need to be great on the outside. Whether you find joy and laughter or pain and sorrow along your journey, be always encouraged. Don't be too hard on yourself. Love yourself, then forgive yourself, and then love yourself some more.

Give yourself permission to be vulnerable and feel all emotions. Even in the worst moments, tell yourself that it is okay to feel the way you do. This is what it means to be human. *All* of this.

Being perfect shouldn't be part of our agenda—only remaining steadfast in all we do is essential to grow into our greater selves.

I can't wait to meet you on the other side.

Your Action Item

This final activity is very simple.

I just want you to do what you do best: be great, smile often and be yourself.

Stay focused and committed through all things. I know you can do it.

Smile in the face of adversity and embrace all challenges head-on. The late, legendary Kobe Bryant once said:

"I have self-doubt. I have insecurities. I have a fear of failure. I have nights when I show up to the arena and I'm like, 'My back hurts, my feet hurt, my knees hurt.' I don't have it. I just want to chill. We all have self-doubt. You don't deny it, but you don't capitulate to it. You embrace it."

Whatever you face, be bold and flexible.

The Grass Isn't Always Greener Mantra

No matter what I find on the other side of my dreams,

I will always be true to myself.

I will not doubt myself.

I will prevail until I reach my destination.

The grass may not be greener on the other side,

But it is beautiful still.

_____

I would never think

in a million years

that the person

I needed most

was

me.

SECTION TWO

Things to Remember

+ Being honest with yourself is about seeing things as they really are, accepting your truth, and making decisions to improve your life.

+ Acceptance is not just seeing with your eyes, but with your heart and soul.

+ If you are willing to put in the work, make the sacrifices and take the losses that provide the necessary experience, you can do anything. I really mean that! Many others have proven it before us.

+ There's no gratification when we only look forward. When we don't take the time to acknowledge and embrace the little things, we miss out on the process that makes us who we are. As we start to disassociate from what made us, we lose ourselves.

+ Be flexible in your approach towards loving yourself and the life you experience. We all have our own journey and our paths are uniquely designed. You already possess everything you need on the inside to be great on the outside.

FINAL THOUGHTS

Wow! I am truly honored to have shared this experience with you.

Believe me when I say that I am wholeheartedly humbled and grateful for your support, and your commitment to give love and adoration to yourself before anyone else. It's the life-force inside all of us.

Once we've given ourselves that vital gift, we will want to help each other to see and embrace it.

It's a funny thing, going on a reality tv show. You get to experience your fifteen minutes of fame, your character is displayed for all the viewers to see and all of your friends and family see all sides of you. (Never entirely pretty!)

Mike Tyson once famously said, "We all have a plan until we get hit."

Recovering from the 10 months of grief after my break-up taught me that what I soak up has a significant effect on me. I stopped listening to music and listened to motivational positive speakers instead. On social media, I don't follow women because of their looks but because of their positivity and the educational information they share. I unfollow people who spew things that aren't good for my soul. This shift in what I consume aided me in so many beautiful ways.

But when I came off the show, I wasn't ready. I wasn't anticipating the amount of overwhelming love, nor the hate and the racist comments. Your level of self-love and self-respect is tested when you have millions of people praising you and hundreds of thousands hating on you. You learn a lot.

When George Floyd was murdered after so many other murders of Black civilians were caught on tape, after so many marches, there was no, "Am I doing and saying the right thing?" I love myself enough not to give a damn what anyone says. I lost a lot of followers because of my Black Lives Matter activism, but I sleep better at night because I follow my heart.

Self-love truly is a belief in oneself that cannot be destroyed by any force.

This book is a major part of me. I've given my heart and my truth, mapping the path that allowed me to grow and that I believe will help you grow too.

Enhancing our minds and stretching our thinking is key to economic freedom. Self-love heals our minds and our hearts, which is key to achieving anything else. By strengthening our minds and learning how to love ourselves, we free ourselves from whatever might hold us back from achieving our greatness.

There are so many people I'm grateful to for helping me get to this point. I was blessed to be raised in such a strong household of courageous women—they taught me countless invaluable life lessons, many that resonate with me still. Their examples were priceless.

I love my sister Amber so much because she's always been herself. She's taught me empathy, patience and understanding. Most importantly, she's taught me that there is more than one way to do right.

Arriving in this place has been monumental.

As I continue to learn and grow, I pray that you all do as well. Together, we have grown and evolved into stronger vessels of self-love. By increasing our self-love, we can each pour our unique blessings into this world.

From my heart, thank you.

Best of luck to you all, no matter what your goals are.

Bae, love yourself.

Made in the USA
Coppell, TX
31 January 2021